T0105268

VICUÑA

Jon Robin Baitz

VICUÑA

A PLAY

FARRAR, STRAUS AND GIROUX | NEW YORK

Farrar, Straus and Giroux
175 Varick Street, New York 10014

Library of Congress Cataloging-in-Publication Data
Names: Baitz, Jon Robin, 1961– author.
Title: Vicuña : a play / Jon Robin Baitz.
Description: First edition. | New York : Farrar, Straus and
    Giroux, [2017]
Identifiers: LCCN 2017016834 | ISBN 9780374283599
    (hardcover) | ISBN 9780374717339 (ebook)
Subjects: LCSH: Presidential candidates—United States—
    Drama. | Political culture—United States—Drama. |
    Tailors—Drama. | Political plays. | GSAFD: Satire.
Classification: LCC PS3552.A393 V53 2017
    | DDC 812/.54—dc23
LC record available at https://lccn.loc.gov/2017016834

Designed by Richard Oriolo

Our books may be purchased in bulk for promotional,
educational, or business use. Please contact your local
bookseller or the Macmillan Corporate and Premium
Sales Department at 1-800-221-7945, extension 5442, or
by e-mail at MacmillanSpecialMarkets@macmillan.com.

www.fsgbooks.com
www.twitter.com/fsgbooks • www.facebook.com/fsgbooks

10 9 8 7 6 5 4 3 2 1

To my husband, Leon Avelino, who reminded me that it can't hurt to love the audience—even when they take phone calls during the show. And to Robert Egan, who still believes.

VICUÑA

CHARACTERS

ANSELM KASSAR

KURT SEAMAN

AMIR MASOUD

SRILANKA SEAMAN

KITTY FINCH-GIBBON

SETTING

New York City: a bespoke tailor's atelier in the east Sixties.

Texas: the debate stage at Baylor University.

The world premiere of *Vicuña* was produced by Center Theatre Group / Kirk Douglas Theatre (Michael Ritchie, Artistic Director) in Los Angeles, California, in 2016. It was directed by Robert Egan. The scenic design was by Kevin Depinet; the costume design was by Laura Bauer; the lighting design was by Tom Ontiveros; and the original music and sound design were by Karl Fredrik Lundeberg. The cast was as follows:

ANSELM KASSAR	Brian George
KURT SEAMAN	Harry Groener
AMIR MASOUD	Ramiz Monsef
SRILANKA SEAMAN	Samantha Sloyan
KITTY FINCH-GIBBON	Linda Gehringer

The Ojai Playwrights Conference (Robert Egan, Artistic Director) workshopped *Vicuña* in August 2016.

(*Early October in Manhattan. A bespoke men's tailor shop on the Upper East Side. It is late afternoon and we are on the second floor of a brownstone in the Sixties. Some street sounds waft up. Large casement windows give out onto the city. An elevator to the ground floor. A drinks cart.*)

(*There are two men in conference.* ANSELM KASSAR, *a tailor, a suit maker, with a shock of flowing white hair and an accent out of some part of Europe we cannot pinpoint precisely, is in a suit and very good shirt, tie, and suspenders, but not wearing the jacket, as he is working. His client is* KURT SEAMAN, *a man in his early sixties, exuding power.*)

ANSELM: You need it when?

SEAMAN: For the final debate, it's November second.

ANSELM: Kurt, are you insane? With all possible—

SEAMAN (*cuts him off*): Anselm, please. Also I only
    have twenty minutes, they're waiting for me at the
    Jewish Council on Primate Development! Can we
    not debate this? I have people downstairs—my
    daughter, her fiancé—

ANSELM: Twenty minutes? Are you stark raving mad?
    I don't do twenty-minute fittings.

SEAMAN: Anselm, just measure me!

ANSELM: A suit normally, the normal number of
    fittings, the process, it's at least three fittings, and
    then many, many adjustments, small ones, corrections
    and more corrections, more consideration. You are
    asking that this be done in three weeks. You are
    asking for an acceleration of a process that is, by its
    nature, slow. *And you've lost your silhouette: your
    waist size has doubled!*

SEAMAN: Yeah, well, you try having a chef who does
    duck à l'orange and gumbo carbonara four nights a
    week! Jesus, Anselm, I know you made a suit for
    President Reagan in less time than that.

ANSELM: Mr. Reagan, he was president. He was Ronald

Reagan! You are not. For a president, you push others aside, and people understand. My clients understood that for Ronald Reagan, they must wait.

SEAMAN: Anselm. It's for the final *debate* watched by *millions*! Come on! Picture it: *I walk across the stage*, I sit on a stool, every network around the world on me. As I cut her to shreds and then win! A great giant cataclysmic operatic huge fucking triumphant win. And in your—in *your* attire! Think how much business you'll get.

ANSELM: The last time I made a suit for you, black tie, gorgeous, to wear to the Met Gala, to wear to the opening of, I believe, the last Balanchine season, but on TV you were wearing a white jacket—*white*— and then you never came back.

SEAMAN: My *second* wife, Cornucopia, she made me.

ANSELM: *You* attempted to return it in a brown paper bag from Bloomingdales—Cornucopia brought it in. Rumpled.

SEAMAN: I divorced her for that—and I have not come to you sooner because, for one, I'm, you know, *busy running for president*, and for *two*, I'm not sure you're even on my side—

ANSELM: Mr. Seaman. I am a bespoke tailor; I have no sides. I am to men's clothes as a doctor is to maladies: I cure the badly attired of the cancer of stylelessness.

I see you on TV, and think, "Why does Kurt
Seaman allow for a collar to hunch, hip to bulge,"
when all of these . . . *idiosyncrasies* of nature and
genetics and *appetite* can be rectified by a master
tailor.

What I see standing here is a man who dresses
like Boris Yeltsin at the opening of a herring factory
in Vladivostok.

SEAMAN (*laughing*): I'm trying to do something. *Please.*
For all of us, for the American people. Plus. Come
on. You made *her* a suit, didn't you?

ANSELM: Kurt. I don't discuss who I—

SEAMAN (*over him*): Yeah, yeah, you did. *And* she
suddenly looked the part. My opponent—*her*
credibility. It—that royal blue—it gave her stature
and made her hips less . . . hip-ish. It made her lies
less—lie-ish. Right? I want that too!

ANSELM: *Yes, this is what clothing does.* Lend credibility.
Authority. But it is too late to do the perfect job
for you.

SEAMAN: This is the election where we finally are
addressing the betrayal, the great betrayal of
millions of hardworking unemployed folks—where
suddenly on every corner it's tacos and weird
Ethiopian soups that you gotta eat with your hands,
while people watch their jobs move to Asia and
Mexico—

ANSELM: Notwithstanding the fact you have a line of
clothes made in *Bangladesh*? Really, Kurt. Please.
SEAMAN: Don't be naïve. So I had a licensing agreement
with someone in Bangladesh, I'm after all a
businessman and America is about business, is it
not, yes it is. Period end of story now what?
(*beat*)
And moreover, I can win. I see what your look says,
the "polls," the *"polling,"* they show me trailing—
well, let me tell you something about me and the
polls: *They lie.* They stink! I had a poll taken about
people who were afraid to admit to their friends
and neighbors that secretly they were on my—on
my side, with me, *under me*—with me—so, so—*it's
much closer than people think.* I need you. You
haven't had a presidential suit since Reagan!
ANSELM (*screams, outraged*): I MADE BUSH'S
JUMPSUIT FOR THE AIRCRAFT CARRIER!
SEAMAN: You will solidify your legacy as the greatest
tailor to the greatest presidents in American
history! You could be really, really rich.

(*And silence.*)

ANSELM: Let me look at the schedule.
SEAMAN: All right! Great!
(ANSELM *peers at a calendar as* AMIR, *his assistant, a*

handsome young fellow in his twenties, comes in, tea for
two on a tray.)

ANSELM: Put it down and leave us.
AMIR: I have tea. I have tea and fancy cookies from
    Poll. Marzipan and ginger.

(AMIR *sets down tea. Looks at* SEAMAN.)

ANSELM (*sharply*): Amir. Please, go down and mind the
    shop, if you will.
AMIR: But. I just wanted to meet Mr. Seaman. In
    person.
ANSELM: This is my apprentice, Amir. Amir Masoud.
    Meet Kurt Seaman.
SEAMAN: "Apprentice." Apprenticeship is good, it's my
    thing, nice to meet you!

(SEAMAN *shakes* AMIR's *hand.*)

AMIR: So, is Mr. Kassar going to build you a suit?
SEAMAN: Yeah, I have the final debate in three weeks,
    it's one of those where you're at a podium, you're on
    a stool, and you walk down to the audience and tell
    them you know exactly what they're going through.
AMIR: In three weeks? How?
SEAMAN: *Fast.* Best suit of all the suits. And not only
    that, I want to offer your boss here a branch of

Anselm de Paris in my hotel in Abu Dhabi and my
hotel in Singapore.

ANSELM (*pleased*): Kurt, how generous.

AMIR: We do this, Anselm, and we get people *very
angry*. It means everything else gets put aside. Suits
for other important and powerful people.

SEAMAN: Is there anyone more important than the
president?

AMIR (*laughs*): Right now, I think almost *anyone* is
more important than the president.

SEAMAN (*laughs with* AMIR): Ah. But I'll be different,
son. I knocked out seventeen losers to become the
candidate and one by one they went down, the Holy
Rollers, the Texan reptile, and a weak-kneed Puerto
Rican immigrant who tried to get into a pissing
contest with me over our manhood, and who was
left standing? Me.

AMIR: A Puerto Rican isn't an immigrant, it's a what-
do-they-call-it? A *protectorate*.

SEAMAN: Thank you. Exactly. But the real question is
protection at what cost? You know what they say
about trying to save a drowning man, son?

AMIR: No . . . What?

SEAMAN: We can't let our country drown because of
the weakness and irresponsibility of our illegal
dependents. Wherever they are. See. The weak can
kill the strong if the strong are too weak to know
when the weak are getting too strong. One way for

the strong to stay strong is to not give in to the weak, who can be very, very strong when cornered.

AMIR: Look at Mr. Kassar here, he's an immigrant, right, who became a citizen—do you want to close the door on men like him? He came here with nothing. America was *good* to him, and he has been good to America.

SEAMAN: Yes. *And*—the same must be true for your parents. They clearly brought up a fine, questioning young fellow, didn't they? Where did they come from, your parents?

AMIR: Iran.

SEAMAN: So many wonderful people there, so many less wonderful people there.

AMIR: Just like here. Right?

SEAMAN: I knew the Shah, he was terrific, I built him a terrific lodge on the Caspian Sea with a terrific terrazzo—were your folks Jewish folk who fled the revolution like Anselm here?

AMIR (*a smile*): No, they're actually Muslim.

SEAMAN: Immigrants?

AMIR: Yes, sir.

SEAMAN: I bet your parents are wonderful. I'd be happy to meet them.

AMIR: They would be very intimidated by you, but I'm sure you would assuage their fears. By your charm. And elegance.

SEAMAN: Oh. I like you, son.

AMIR: I like you, too, sir.

(to ANSELM*)*

> But I've got to say, I don't think we have the time to make as good a suit as Mr. Seaman would need in so little time.

SEAMAN: Anselm, you made my father's first suit after he closed his biggest deal, 1974. Adolf Z. Seaman. You were his man.

> He pulled you out of apprenticeship and made you a tailor. Back when you were in Brooklyn. Both of you. Authentic people. And that's what I believe in—authentic American people: John Wayne, John Ford, Winston Churchill. *That* is why I have come to you. I never forget my friends, *you know this!*

ANSELM (*finally, a decision*): Amir. Please. Bring me up the vicuña we just got from London.

AMIR: Really? Isn't that spoken for? The Sultan of—

ANSELM (*cuts him off, edgy*): Please.

(to SEAMAN*)*

> English vicuña. And pashmina, and qiviut. It's very special.

(to AMIR, *a warning*)

> Go. Now. Please.

(AMIR *nods and leaves.*)

SEAMAN: Huh. Great kid, lot of personality. Smart, too.

ANSELM: He lacks silence. A certain kind of work
   requires silence.
SEAMAN (*a blustery guffaw*): Monks, accountants,
   hookers, and librarians, yeah. And bespoke tailors?
ANSELM: This is very serious. You understand, a vicuña
   suit, if you go to Loro Piana or Kiton, or one of the
   guys on Savile Row—a made-to-measure suit of this
   kind is unspeakably expensive. Everything is hand
   stitched, nothing by machine.
SEAMAN: You know I got—
ANSELM (*cuts him off, sharp*): Please let me finish!
   You've never spent this kind of money on clothing,
   if you go to Zegna, it's—and I promise you, make
   one call, you will see—it's *forty-eight thousand
   dollars* for the most affordable one. Mine will be
   much more because I have to drop other people's
   work, and explain to them for the first time in
   my entire working life, forty years, I shall be not
   on time. The chairman of Nestlé at a conference
   on the future of water and why it should not
   be free.
(*beat*)
   It doesn't matter who you are, one does not do
   what you are asking, because you see, Kurt, *my
   people succeed*. Like your father did before you. Is
   it magic, a magic trick, is it *mystical*, is it some
   atavistic force? I don't know. I only know that if you
   want a suit for the great debate, it is going to cost you

one hundred and fifty thousand dollars including of course two shirts and two ties. And what? Can I guarantee that you will win the election in my suit? No. But I can promise you this: The day of the debate, the day of November second, those on the fence who see you will be *swayed,* those who have judged will *reconsider,* those who *love you* will love you *more. So.* The next word out of your mouth is either "yes" or "no"!

(SEAMAN *decides.*)

SEAMAN: Yes. You have a deal.
ANSELM: Take out your credit card. Now. I'll begin at once.

(SEAMAN *takes out a black card and* ANSELM *swipes it.*)

SEAMAN: I have to say, I don't remember you being quite so good at this, maybe you should be my secretary of commerce.
(*He takes a piece of paper out of his breast pocket*)
And here is my standard nondisclosure, as someone in business with me, everyone signs this.
ANSELM (*signing*): All of my clients are afforded the same level of discretion.
SEAMAN: And it applies to *all* of your employees as well.

(The elevator door opens with a PING and AMIR *returns.)*

AMIR: Here. Vicuña. Look at it.
(He lays it out)
>   Up in the Andes, pretty much the only place you
>   find them. Peru, part of Argentina, and a bit of
>   Bolivia. The vicuña, little cousin to the llama. It
>   had been poached for centuries. Right? Dying
>   out. A great animal that we decimated to virtual
>   extinction.

ANSELM: Worn only at first by Incan royalty, then in
>   the 1500s King Philip of Spain slept under a vicuña
>   blanket, this gorgeous fiber, the very finest hair on
>   the planet, the diameter of which is thirteen point
>   five microns, as opposed to, say, cashmere, which is
>   fourteen to seventeen point five. Yeah.
>
>   Lighter than air, warmer than a dozen layers of
>   wool but breathes like nothing else.

AMIR: Yeah, at FIT they taught us you can never be
>   thoughtless with this, it's as if you were a brain
>   surgeon. It's too valuable to make mistakes. Never
>   worked with it before, myself, but you, boss? A
>   Rockefeller.

ANSELM: Nelson. And I used it for one other suit, worn
>   by Sir Roger Moore, the best Bond, *Octopussy.*
>   This dark navy, see it, and the pinstripe, an inch
>   apart.

SEAMAN: I am awed. I am thrilled. Which is the least I can expect from a hundred-and-fifty-thousand-dollar suit.

AMIR (*gobsmacked*): One hundred and fifty thousand?

(ANSELM *is pleased.*)

SEAMAN (*looking, examining*): In a suit made of this, how could I lose?

ANSELM (*serious*): Kurt. You must make yourself available for *all* fittings. After all, what is a suit? A suit is more than cloth and stitching, it is a glimpse into the soul of a man. The interior life of a man is glimpsed only in two moments—when he makes love—

SEAMAN (*testing*): To a *woman*?

ANSELM: Perhaps. And when he dresses.

(*The elevator PINGs, a young woman in her twenties enters, so styled that it's breathtaking.* SEAMAN'*s daughter* SRILANKA.)

SRILANKA: Dad! You're gonna be late for CAIKE.

SEAMAN: Let me guess, the Christian Action—

SRILANKA (*over him*): No, Dad, *CAIKE:* the Committee of American/Israeli Conservative Executives!

(AMIR *stifles a snort of laughter.*)

SRILANKA: And then there's a meeting with MUMU—
the Munitions Makers' Union—after the CAIKE
speech, which I think we should actually cancel.
Why? Because I really need to start prepping
you for your speech to the Barnard Republican
Association.
SEAMAN (*gets it right finally*): BRA.
SRILANKA: Yes. Hi. Welcome to Thursday!

(AMIR *suppresses another laugh.*)

SEAMAN: Everyone, this is Srilanka, my beautiful
daughter, I'm sure you've seen her on TV, at my
side, never has anyone had a better campaign
manager.
(*beat*)
Why do you keep pushing this BRA speech?
(*sees her hesitate*)
We are among friends.
SRILANKA (*very focused and loving*): You're *still* weakest
with white suburban women, educated ones, and
mothers, and you can't win without them! They have
to see the man who removed the glass ceiling a *long
time ago*, the man who respects them and gives them
opportunities. And for you to give that speech at
my alma mater, a bastion of East Coast liberal
thought, you must be thoughtful, sober, and
gracious. The best version of yourself, the man *I*

know. That is vital, Dad. Our message is being diluted when you aren't disciplined.

SEAMAN (*hugs her*): Yes. But, darling, you gotta *let me be me*, or else the people who elect me won't be electing the man who they thought they selected to elect. How's the CAIKE speech coming?

SRILANKA: You talk about how "neoliberalism" has become code for old-school anti-Semitism, then you talk about how many settlements you'd finance as president, about my fiancé, Schuyler Ironson, and how I converted to Judaism.

AMIR: Let me guess—you finish with a joke about how many Jews does it take to change a lightbulb?

SRILANKA (*smiles*): Yes! Maybe you should come work for the campaign.

SEAMAN (*smiling, to* AMIR): Oh, *come on*, what? Amir? Let me ask you. As a man from *Iran*, does my friendship with—my deep loyalty to—Israel, does that *bother* you?

AMIR: Of course not. I have Jewish friends. *I'm a New Yorker.* We're *all* Jewish, no matter what. New York does that to you. The angst.

(SEAMAN *laughs.*)

ANSELM: Let's think about what sort of cut we're going to do, I think more American than English—

SEAMAN (*cuts him off; to* AMIR): You have a sense of

[19]

humor. As much as I value skills and hard work, social ease is just as important.

(*to* SRILANKA)

I *love* this kid.

(*to* AMIR)

So. You are going to work *with* Anselm, yes? Shoulder to shoulder? Deep into the wee small hours? Yes? Son?

(*Holds jazz hands aloft*)

Keep it all jazzy and with it and a little young? New blood, Anselm—like Srilanka, right? You have Amir, I have her!

SRILANKA: Dad. Listen. Schuyler is downstairs and needs to go over your meeting with BORCHT.

SEAMAN: Help me.

SRILANKA: Brotherhood of Republican Conservative Hebrew Teachers! And also Mom texted and said her book club in Santa Barbara are asking why you hate women. This is what I'm talking about with the Barnard speech. Women do not trust you!

SEAMAN: Oh, come on! Women love Seaman and Seaman loves women!

AMIR: That's *exactly* the answer to give at the debate about your position on women.

(SRILANKA *laughs.* SEAMAN *looks at* AMIR. *Her phone rings; she takes it and moves upstage.*)

SEAMAN (*laughing but dangerous*): Not many people poke fun at me, Amir. It's nice. I like it. It's novel. Anselm, let's go look at ties, shall we?

ANSELM (*hits the elevator button*): By all means. Please. Amir, rearrange the schedule and clean up here, please.

SEAMAN: Srilanka?

SRILANKA (*holds phone to chest*): I'll be right there, just finishing up this call.

(*Doors open with a PING.* ANSELM *and* SEAMAN *get in the elevator.* AMIR *tidies up.* SRILANKA *gets off the phone.*)

AMIR: So. It must be hard being the campaign manager for your own father. When he's so unpredictable.

SRILANKA: He listens to me. It takes some work, but he trusts me more than anyone else.

AMIR: Do you think he'll take your counsel when he goes to Barnard to prove . . . he's a new man?

SRILANKA: He decided something about me very early. That I was going to represent the best version of him, and so I tried to not prove him wrong. He hates disappointing me, so, yes. I think he will.

AMIR: We shall see.

SRILANKA (*taking in suits*): How do you do it? These suits? It feels like sort of a magic act to me.

AMIR: Magic? Nope. It's just craft, it's like anything done by hand, Ms. Seaman.

SRILANKA: You, really, you can call me Srilanka. I'm sorry. I guess saying it's magic is a little bit . . . blithe.

AMIR (*charmed*): Only slightly.

(*gingerly*) But. I mean. Srilanka? Is that an actual name?

SRILANKA: An actual name from an actual place. Have you been there?

AMIR: Just this past week, in fact. I have barely unpacked.

SRILANKA (*laughs*): I was, it seems, conceived there. You know. Dad built a resort there. You know we want to put bespoke tailoring in some of the properties? Well?

AMIR (*smart and fun*): What, you'd go on a seven-day vacation, get measured up, and bang: walk out with your suit, made by cheapo labor in a sweatshop where children work day and night to accommodate bloated tourists who've spent the week baking themselves in the sun and eating "exotic" dishes.

SRILANKA: *Yes.* Your suit is ready by the time you leave.

AMIR: Do you know *how* stupid that sounds?

SRILANKA: Well, it wouldn't be like this, here, like this level of the work you guys do here—

AMIR (*delightfully provocative*): No, it wouldn't, because

nothing is like this; this is labor, this is sculpting. The pattern on paper, brown paper. It's no different from drafting a building. The body in question, say, that of your dad, right? You do these calculations, and use rulers and tools, the french curve—

(*He reaches for a curved metal implement, a ruler*)

You join all the lines, the positions, measuring, more measuring. Tiny corrections. Half of this number is this position, half of that number is where the armhole is, and so on. Do you know how hard it is to get an armhole exactly right?

(*He smiles, with holiness*)

One uses canvas, good canvas, it is the foundation of the jacket, canvas with a bit of weight. It gives the jacket shape, for the chest, say. Then the lining, chosen for mood. I like silk. All of it, you know, hand sewn, of course. You do the basting, the infinite measurements for armholes, the hundreds of stitches. All before the first fitting.

(*Drily gestures to the form*)

Ta-da. "Magic." *That's* your magic.

SRILANKA: Wow. You *really* don't care for us. You think we don't know what real work is?

AMIR: I'm sorry. I don't know you. *You*, I don't know.

SRILANKA: You are right. You don't know me. *Me*, you don't know. But *him*, of course, you *do*.

AMIR: Your father is on every possible media outlet

from the moment one awakens to the moment one finally fitfully falls asleep, so I think I do know him. And in person he is very charming, magnetic, but I have the slight impression that he's maybe slightly delusional?

SRILANKA (*confrontational*): You can't go around saying things like that. This is a confidential relationship between a man and his tailor. You— just work here.

AMIR: Until he becomes president, actually, I *can*. After that, well, Guantánamo is gonna get pretty crowded, I think.

SRILANKA: My father is loyal to the people he loves, and he loves them deeply, he's helped thousands of people, he's built businesses, he's got to play ball with the people you find disgusting but you'll find that he's—once elected—going to be far more humane than the man he's been painted as.

(*quick beat*)

You seem smart enough to understand a daughter's loyalty. Do you love *your* father?

AMIR: More than I can say, yes, both of my parents.

SRILANKA: Well, then you must know that your derision about mine is actually more than a little offensive, and I am struggling to be civil with you.

AMIR: You needn't be civil, Srilanka: It's your honesty that makes you so interesting. Civil people are often *the* most awful ones.

SRILANKA: You know a lot about awful people?
AMIR: This is New York, we're all awful.

(*A PING. The elevator opens.* ANSELM *steps out.*)

ANSELM: Srilanka, my dear, your father is downstairs.
Waiting.
SRILANKA: Thank you. I'm sure you're going to build
him something very special.
(*to* AMIR)
It was nice meeting you.
AMIR: Oh. Yes. Very.

(*She gets into the elevator; the door closes.*)

ANSELM: *I need a drink.* Yes. I can see you do not
approve.

(ANSELM *goes to the drinks cart and pours them both
vodka.*)

AMIR: He's sort of a wonder to behold, like a kraken or
a four-headed goat glowing green outside a nuclear
reactor. Anselm, *are you joking*? He's a *monster*!
ANSELM (*a shrug*): So, even monsters need clothing. If
you wish to be a suit maker, you cannot concern
yourself with the niceties and gradations of their
philosophies.

AMIR: So, wait: You would dress a man responsible
for actual evil, a Hitler maybe, a Pol Pot, a
Saddam?

ANSELM: What makes you think that I did not spend
three days in the Hotel Negresco in Nice fitting
Idi Amin for new Nehru jackets?

AMIR: Idi Amin?

ANSELM: I was civilizing him so that when he looked in
the mirror he had the opportunity to see the better
angels of his nature.

AMIR: You sound like fucking Coco Chanel!

ANSELM: It is free enterprise that maketh a society
great! And this one principle is the overriding one
that Kurt Seaman adheres to. You were not alive
during the terrible years of Jimmy Carter. He did
not come to me—he who dressed in the vestments
of sorrow, of guilt, of the mendicant—speaking of a
great "malaise" which was in fact willed into being
by his own contorted moralizing. So he had lust in
his heart—big deal, *this* is a news flash? Who doesn't?

AMIR: I do. I had like twenty J-Lo posters on my wall.
"Don't be fooled by the rocks that I got, I'm still
Jenny from the block."

ANSELM: It is lust that makes a man—that is why we
pay extra attention when we sew the crotch!
There should be just the slight suggestion of
something—a small tiny pregnancy in the loin

area—to convey that a man is a man! Seaman is filled with lust—and lust makes for good men and good leaders.

AMIR: But Anselm, right now, what is happening, Seaman . . . the man is calling for deportations, he is calling for people—my people—to be stripped systematically of their rights. "All Muslims should be deported."

ANSELM: It's all talk, it's sales, it's hucksterism.

AMIR: My father, he's struggled to cobble together five hot dog carts sprinkled around midtown. You know this, you bought him his first. *How is he a threat to anyone?* My parents are terrified.

ANSELM: Yes, and you have to be prudent.

AMIR: Anselm. He said on CNN one in four of us is a violent *jihadist*! He is like a giant machine that makes evil disgusting bloated nasty doughnuts. Anything anyone throws at him, he turns it into a batter to make a doughnut with! And eats it. And spits it back.

ANSELM: I cannot, will not, be drawn into one of your screeds, this is a screed-free zone, absent of lectures and *geschrei-ing*!—

(*beat*)

You goaded him today and virtually mocked him to his face.

AMIR: I didn't bow and scrape to him, no!

ANSELM: You have such contempt for caution. What an American luxury.

AMIR: In America, it's safe to call bullshit!

ANSELM: Before you judge us who have walked away from politics, you might consider how that right was earned. When your father and I were at university together and I spoke out against the Shah, SAVAK came after my whole family. They accused me of being a Communist, a terrorist. And they killed my brother to get to me. Your father gave me the money to get to Paris. He saved my life. And I made a promise to never put anyone at risk again through word or deed. And you've made a promise?

You scared your parents rather more than Kurt Seaman is scaring them. What was that promise?

AMIR (*quietly*): To find discipline and order and a path for a future.

ANSELM: You no longer have the collegiate luxury of running naked through Harvard Yard *covered in goat blood*, waving a burning American flag, every time there is a *drone strike* somewhere. Recklessness is not for the children of immigrants.

Recklessness is the privilege of spoiled American children.

(*major avuncular advice*)

And don't flirt with his daughter. I know it's your natural state, I know this, but please, I saw it.

AMIR: Sorry.

ANSELM: Yeah. "Sorry." Don't try to look innocent.

(AMIR *smiles. He loves this man.*)

AMIR: You think flirting is a crime, too? Okay. It's just a way to make the day better, dude.

(ANSELM *nods.*)

ANSELM: Listen, darling. I don't mind if you pick up one of the bored housewives of Manhattan who float in here on a cloud of Chanel and Klonopin, but *please*, leave Srilanka Seaman alone. Really.

AMIR (*laughs*): Stop. Please. God. I get it.

ANSELM: Drink up, my boy. You're learning great things here. Great things . . . *L'chaim*. To life.

(ANSELM *and* AMIR *down their shots.*)

END OF ACT ONE, SCENE ONE

(*It is October. A week later. We are in the atelier. The partially built suit on a model. A gorgeous navy pinstripe. It's incomplete, with white stitching all over it.*)

(SRILANKA *inspects it. There is a PING, and* AMIR *enters.*)

AMIR: Hello.
(*re the suit*)
   So? Thoughts? Questions? Comments?
SRILANKA: Hi. Well. It's very presidential. But. It seems like a hundred-and-fifty-thousand-dollar suit might *do* more, like ventriloquism or making an omelette.

AMIR: Ah, but it's *not* a hundred-and-fifty-thousand-dollar suit; it's a forty-five-thousand-dollar suit that mowed down more *patient* suits on its way to the buffet.

(*beat*)

Srilanka. I am sorry for my terrible manners when you were here last.

SRILANKA (*engaged, and not ungrateful*): I actually didn't mind all that much. It's always nice *not* to be lied to; people think you can't *tell*. I can always tell.

AMIR: But still, I was wrong. And you must be having an effect on your dad: I heard bits of his Barnard speech on CNN. He was gentlemanly and decent and reasonable to women. He was recognizable as a human. Did you tranquilize him? Sorry!

SRILANKA: He did well. He did not veer into some kind of impulsive female ad hominem, and the response has been great, and may I have some vodka?

(*She goes to the drinks cart and pours herself a healthy shot.*)

AMIR: Is everything okay?

SRILANKA: Yes, sorry, I just have so much to keep track of. The debate prep. Yes, the reaction has been everything we needed: "The great empowerment of women!" he called it. You know, his raised minimum wage for single mothers—

AMIR (*smiling*): Well. You must stay by his side, at all
    times? Especially if he does win. He will need you.

SRILANKA: God knows.

AMIR: We all will.

SRILANKA: May I ask you something, please?

AMIR: Please. Anything.

SRILANKA: You're not a journalist, right?

AMIR: What?

SRILANKA: You just don't fit the mold, the image of a
    tailor. It's not just your erudition, of course, I know
    many erudite makers of clothes. But you seem like
    the product of a particular kind of education.

AMIR: What kind of particular education, Srilanka?

SRILANKA: An expensive one.

AMIR: Ah. Well. Yes.

SRILANKA (*smiles, wry*): You see, people have posed as
    employees to get closer to us. When I was twelve we
    had a cook who turned out to be a plant from
    Rolling Stone. His turducken was a lot better than
    the piece he wrote about our family Christmas
    dinner.

AMIR: Well. Christmas in *Queens* was always very
    simple. No fake chefs and turducken—

SRILANKA (*studying him*): So what is it, then? I know
    your parents were immigrants. And they wanted
    you to succeed. So how did that lead to here?

AMIR: How did I get my expensive education and then
    become an apprentice suit maker?

SRILANKA: I just don't quite get it. It's not public school and City College. You're too . . . you're like someone who had a serious education. You quit something before ending up here, didn't you?

AMIR (*impressed*): Wow. Now *that* is a magic act. How'd you do that? I was plucked out of public school in fifth grade by a foundation that takes minority kids and sends them to very good, very expensive private schools. Trinity! And then, after the perfect grades and captain of the fencing team and debate, how could they not let me into *Harvard*!

SRILANKA: One of my brothers went to Trinity.

AMIR: I know. Lucas.

SRILANKA: *You know Lucas?*

AMIR: *Knew.* He'd probably not remember me, I was in eleventh grade and he was in eighth. I helped him with soccer.

(*delighted contempt*)

Now Lucas shoots defenseless lions and elephants in game parks in Africa, of course. *So*, sportsmanship was clearly not a lesson he learned among the blue bloods of Gotham. I bet all the kids I went to school with are dying for your father to be their president because it simply validates their greed and lack of kindness. All those kids who are now bloated bond traders, they must really love your dad and his deregulation and tax breaks for the rich.

SRILANKA: I'm not going to debate capitalism with you, really, Amir. It's pointless, it's not even fun. It isn't sexy either, by the way. And plus, what are you doing here making suits for the elite, then?

AMIR (*smiles, laughs, caught*): Never heard of a Marxist tailor? It's very French. Paris is *full* of 'em.

(*quietly*)

I met your dad back then, he'd never remember, of course, he came to pick up Lucas one day, and we were on the soccer field, watching Lucas practice, and he was divorcing Lucas's mom. And suddenly he started crying about how hard it was to be a good dad. I liked him then. I did. In that moment. Of vulnerability. I didn't know what to do. With your dad. I patted his back. He stopped crying as soon as I touched him.

SRILANKA: And then you *left* Harvard to become a *tailor.*

AMIR: Two years into my master's at the Kennedy School of Government, I was asked to leave. There were acts of protest, performances. I gave them no choice. I was glad. I'd seen enough.

(*beat*)

And I always loved clothes. Specifically a good suit. I loved that they made you somehow more serious. In that, and probably *only* that, I agree with your father.

(*beat*)

My dad has hot dog carts. He never wears a suit. He
did back in Iran. He'd been an elementary school
principal. As a kid I used to put on his old suits, as
he had no use for them anymore, in America. With
his hot dog carts.

(*beat*)

Anselm and my dad were college roommates in
Iran—a Jew and a Muslim. It was a sitcom back then.
Anselm made a suit for me when I was a teenager, a
suit for a prom, and I came here and watched him
make it. It stayed with me. So. Maybe I can't change
the world as a tailor, but that might be what appeals
to me. All my life the pressure to become some sort
of "Important Man" has been unbearable. My
parents think I might become a sort of giant,
a Tom Ford. *I could.* Easily, actually. Suit maker.
I like that it's a form of art and does no harm.
    Usually.

SRILANKA: But not in this case?

AMIR (*quietly direct*): *You bet.* Building a suit to help
persuade the world that Kurt Seaman is the *only*
answer to all their problems. That's not a benign
act. Sorry.

SRILANKA (*fiercely direct*): *So* well articulated. *So* well
expressed. Your people come here from a place
where people are executed for speaking out. And

they are welcomed here! So they come to start anew, and want all of their dreams to come true in you.

They pour into you the best education, the nurturing of your intellect, and then, like so many who have come here from your part of the world, forgive me, you end up spewing very well structured verbal venom: this American viper's nest of end-stage capitalism and greed and ugliness. And you wonder why people like my father want loyalty oaths and investigations?

AMIR: Loyalty oaths? And investigations? Please!

(*There is a moment. She doesn't know what to say. Gets another drink.*)

SRILANKA: I have a little cabin on a lake in Vermont. Far from here. It has no phone, no Internet, just a bed, a nice stove, and some books. It's a secret. I keep saying "go there." Some little voice. On bad days. On days like today.

AMIR: What happened?

SRILANKA: I'm still trying to figure that out.

(*beat*)

My father just finished taping an interview for Fox News. It's going to break in a little bit. It will run . . . in a constant loop.

(*She pulls out her cell phone.*)

SEAMAN (*recorded*): "Listen, Sean, yeah—everything I
said at Barnard, that applies to a particular kind of
woman, but you've got Muslim women, you know,
flooding into the country brainwashing these guys
to strap bombs on their chest. Look at that little
town in California, right? This is a thing! You
know, it's a known thing. So we need loyalty
oaths—for these women! What about that doesn't
make sense, Sean? And Mexican women, they're
coming in—they're taking jobs—I see them at
Carl's Jr. I see them at Jack in the Box, I see them at
Chick-fil-A—"

(*A beat.*)

SRILANKA: My cabin on this lake is looking very good
right now.
AMIR: So. He did that thing—where he gives something
to one group and then he goes to Fox and negates
the entire Barnard speech?
SRILANKA: He didn't negate the Barnard speech. He
nuked it. And I arranged it. I went up there and
introduced him. Me!
AMIR: What are you going to do?
SRILANKA: Please understand this: I am the only

[38]

person who can shake him back into some state that perceives reality as it really is.

AMIR: Come on. *Srilanka.* Do you know what happens if you eat too much caviar? There's so much salt in it, you can no longer taste the wonderful odd fishiness of it. I fear you've had so much caviar that you can no longer taste anything fishy. The Seamans are a corporation, and now it wants to add the White House to its list of Seaman properties. You are part of the team negotiating this takeover.

SRILANKA (*a tough smile*): I actually hate caviar, Amir.

AMIR: My parents are at risk. He could deport them. He could take everything from them. Is that funny to you? Do you get off somehow on being so very close to the source of all that power? Yes? My God, yes, you and your absurd fiancé—sorry, but he is— Schuyler Ironson. Orthodox Jew, son of a psychotic real estate mogul, two empires entwined. You are all so strange to me, the lives you live, the mergers and acquisitions.

SRILANKA: Why are we discussing my engagement to Schuyler Ironson?

AMIR: I am trying to understand if there's any part of you that is authentic. What is it you love in him?

SRILANKA: He's brilliant. He just bought *The New York Beacon.* He's going to make it matter again. Change it from pink to a more salmon color.

AMIR: A bold first step.

SRILANKA: He's buying *"HEY YOU!"* And *The National Epiphany.* He's bought Sporty dot com.

(*tired*)

> He's buying all the media. And he has become my father's most fervent disciple. They are going to start a media empire together after all this. Seaman News!

(*She shakes her head: dark*)

> They've already won is the thing, you see. My dad and Schuyler have won. Kurt Seaman doesn't have to become *the president,* he's now become the *alternative to everything else,* the repository of all the rage, the collector of our national grudge. And that grudge, yes, it's the size of a plague of locusts. Do you think if my father loses, those people are going to simply disappear? He's *unleashed* them!

(*very dark*)

> Every day I do this my jaw aches, my muscles are so taut, I can't sleep. My heart hurts. My friends back away, find me slightly soiled, and wander to the other side of the room at cocktail parties. Schuyler—he stopped loving me as he fell more and more in love with my father and his power. I am alone. Not a day goes by on this campaign where compassion and goodness are even considered. While what America needs right now is the best

version of my dad—the builder, the visionary, the great outsider who isn't afraid of exploding gridlock and saving this country.

AMIR: What do you want?

SRILANKA: What do I want? I just want to prevent a catastrophe, a cataclysm, and restore some decency, some grace to how this is playing out—before my heart breaks completely.

AMIR: Finally. It's simple. Speak out. Then go to your cabin, and read and sleep.

SRILANKA: That is not the most effective use of whatever capital I have!

AMIR: What else can you do? Admit his dark brilliance is code. He speaks hate code to two utterly opposed groups. He gets poor folks who are furious at America—for good reason—to align with the rich folks, and they all hate and blame the government that the rich folks control. It's genius!

And very, very dangerous.

SRILANKA: You should go into politics.

AMIR: Yeah, America is so ready for a Marxist Muslim congressman. You could stop him. If you love this country. Denounce him. Denounce his candidacy.

(*She goes for another drink*)

You know what? In lieu of you going all Amelia Earhart and disappearing, I'd like to make you a suit. A real made-in-America, made-in–New York

City *suit*. A kind of gorgeous gray: éminence-grise gray. A gift.

SRILANKA: Or—a bribe?

AMIR: Ahh, my little turducken. You've been trained to suspect any interest in you.

SRILANKA (*walks toward him*): It's kept me one step ahead of the people we deal with. I know what they're thinking before they do. I can tell by their eyes, my one small superpower.

AMIR: Oh. I think you probably have more than one. (*Studies her*)

A suit for a formidable woman. No better task for a designer.

(*He examines someone possessed of great beauty*)

I'll design it myself just for you. I'll join all the lines, the positions, measuring, more measuring. Tiny corrections. Do you know how hard it is to get the neck exactly right?

Just right? A perfect white shirt. Maybe then you would have the courage to confront your father. One could certainly get behind that.

(*He touches her face. Gently.*)

SRILANKA: What are you doing?

AMIR: I'm examining my conclusion that, to my surprise, and even awe, actually, you value some things more than the Seaman ascendancy. And I think they are things I value too.

(*The moment is about recognition, and seeing past the here and the now. She pulls away.*)

SRILANKA: Well, now you know, don't you.

(*The elevator door PINGs.* SRILANKA *and* AMIR *separate quickly.* ANSELM *and* KURT *exit the elevator.* ANSELM *is carrying a number of shirts and ties.*)

ANSELM (*cheerful*): Hello, we've chosen shirts and ties! A rainbow coalition of color. Red, white, blue, and a royal crimson, it's magic!
SEAMAN (*exuberant*): I'm gonna look fabulous! Incredibly amazing, fabulous, you're not gonna *believe* it! Hello, darling.
SRILANKA: Hi, Dad.

(SEAMAN *sees the suit on the mannequin.*)

SEAMAN: Ooohhhh. And now. And now—it's the suit! The great day!
ANSELM: This is but the first fitting. It's not what it will be. But the outline is there, the form.
SEAMAN: I can already tell. This is going to get me the

election, Anselm. I can always tell what kind of
building is going to be successful, I can tell the
moment the skeleton goes up. It's a winner.

(*He circles the mannequin*)

This suit. Talk about a surrogate. A lot better than that
lox they made me take on for a veep—Pete Quince. I
should send the suit out there instead of *him*!

(*to* AMIR)

Is there a drink? Hi there. *Amin,* is it?

AMIR: Sir, hi, yes, Mr. Seaman—but *Amir.* Scotch,
rocks, I believe?

(AMIR *goes to the drinks cart, pours him a tumbler of
scotch on the rocks.*)

SEAMAN: Anselm, let's try it on. Please.

(ANSELM *carefully takes the coat off the mannequin.*
SEAMAN *puts it on.*)

SEAMAN: Darling, I think I'd like to skip the debate
prep tonight. Marta has made some sort of Bavarian
noodle dish with goose livers and gooseberries and—a
crème brûlée vanilla Sacher torte for dessert. And
I'll order a clam pizza and Schuyler and Svetlana
could come over and we could play Monopoly or
something—

(*to* ANSELM *and* AMIR)

You boys, too, if you like.

ANSELM: Oh, how kind, I love Monopoly, the trick is to take the railroads, you can't lose.

SRILANKA: Dad, we're not skipping prep. It's two weeks to the debate.

SEAMAN: At the last two debates, I did not have this suit. I can assure you, I'll be prepared for her droning lectures on global interdependencies and the importance of being sensitive to the bathroom habits of the emperor of Japan! No, I'm ready for her now, and she can't talk about my attitude to women anymore, not after my brilliant Barnard speech!

SRILANKA: Which you just entirely refuted on Fox, which is actually airing right now. In which you amend everything you promised: "These great equalities must be earned by proving you can work as hard as the strongest man on the team, harder!" In which you mandate, "The women of ISIS. Embedded in our cities. Turning homegrown immigrant children into brainwashed zombie psychopathic shooting bombers. These women must claim loyalty to the United States of America!"

SEAMAN: I was being sarcastic, but—it's not the worst idea, and you know it, and everyone else is afraid to say it! Come *on*. Why not claim your loyalty to the

United States of America? What the fuck's wrong
with that?

SRILANKA: And "Mexican women can't be protected
because they are stealing the jobs of American
women." Where? Where is that happening? Not to
mention it is unconstitutional and antithetical to
American ideals.

(*yelling*)

SO NO! You CANNOT skip debate prep for
gooseberry Sacher torte and fucking clam pizza,
Dad. Don't make the mistake of imagining that
somehow this suit is all you need. You are
forgetting what happened at the last two debates.

AMIR: Not good nights for you, sir.

SEAMAN (*to* AMIR *and* SRILANKA): Let me have it both
barrels, please: What *was* I like, in your opinion, at
the last two debates. Amir? Tell me. Really.

(*There is a silence.*)

AMIR: I think you should have been more respectful of
the principles that gave birth to this country.
Principles that need to be honored now more than
ever.

SEAMAN: Such as?

ANSELM (*firm*): Look. Guys. Really. I *do* have another
fitting, it's gala and benefit season here in this

town, fall, people have the *Met*, the Central Park
Conservancy—
(*at his appointment book*)

I'd love to host a salon, but . . . there are other
people—Barry Diller's on his way.

SEAMAN: Please, Anselm, just another moment, this
man is speaking from the heart, and he's not afraid,
and it's very rare—very rare—to encounter it.
(*earnest*)

Go on, Amir. What principles am I not hitting—for
the debate—what?

SRILANKA (*looking at her phone*): Dad, we don't have
time for this—we are in crisis.

SEAMAN: Please.

AMIR: "All men are created equal." The vision of an
America committed to the repair of the damage
done to that idea. That we're all equal. The old way
of at least letting people enter its *gates* to make their
lives. Maybe where the Bill of Rights and, say, the
Ten Commandments intersect?

When you started, Mr. Seaman, your
improvisatory freedom was bracing. I understood
it. But, excuse me, *a suit*—sir, a suit cannot stand in
for actual *goodness and vision*.

SEAMAN: Huh. Wow. I'm really, I'm surprised.
(*exquisitely articulate*)

How naïve. Son. The America you've somehow

imagined, it never existed other than in bad movies and children's history books. I say this because it would please me to see you really succeed in this ruthless world. It really would.

(*to* SRILANKA)

He's gonna have a lot of trouble, don't you think?

(*beat*)

There is only one American dream now. And it is to simply take what is left. Do you understand? That's all there is now. The angry people understand that. "Take whatever you can, take that which is not nailed down before someone else does."

(*beat*)

But you two fuckers do know how to make a suit.

(*He looks in the mirror. Inspired!*)

In a suit like this, you could do anything.

(*simple*)

It's the great closer. It closes the deal with the American voter.

(*Turns to the imaginary debate audience*)

In this suit, I can say to her with utter authority, "All of your lies, all of your evasions, all of your privilege, your cronyism, the backroom deals you make, your deep, deep contempt and superiority, your faults! Your FAULTS!"

(*beat*)

> "While the banks were working like dark Satanic mills—selling and reselling mortgages as though the American people were merely ink on a ledger—your actions were in the interest of your cronies, and the banks you whispered 'truths' to—while you whispered 'sweet nothings' in the ears of the American people."

(*beat*)

> "Faults! Your carelessness with security is simply a metaphor for how little you care about *our* security. Faults? God, you have so many, but the worst is that you are uninspiring and the American people need to be inspired. And you who are too afraid to use words like 'radical Islamic terrorism,' always finding middle ground between two equidistant groups of mediocrity. You are not in any way fit to serve as the American president."

(*beat*)

> Anselm, there's something about this suit.

ANSELM (*breaking the spell*): Downstairs, I have a pair of cuff links, presidential cuff links given to me by ex-president Richard Nixon when he was in exile in San Clemente. I made him a suit to cheer him up. They're twelve thousand dollars. Let's go see. Amir, I need you to go to Thirty-Eighth Street and find me some grosgrain in black, please, nine yards.

SEAMAN (*catching the dismay*): What is it, son? Don't tell me a man like you believes in what she's selling! I can see how smart you are.

SRILANKA (*checking her phone*): Dad. The chairwoman of the RNC is desperate to talk to you about the Fox interview.

(*She holds her phone, which is buzzing like a Catherine wheel*)

And . . . and . . . shit—oh, no. No. Nobu just pulled out of our hotel in Panama City.

SEAMAN (*shocked*): No, no, not *Nobu!* The rat!

(*turns to* AMIR, *icy*)

Amir, don't leave. Please don't leave. I wanna ask you a question, son. Do you object to my stance on the Muslim problem in America?

AMIR (*controlled*): I know, sir, that you derive some strange satisfaction from trying to make me engage with you, but I have no opinion one way or the other in the atelier.

SEAMAN: Is that possible? You are the son of immigrants from Iran. And what is their status here? Naturalized? Green cards?

AMIR (*even more controlled*): Their status, sir, is none of your concern.

SRILANKA (*looks at her phone*): Well, Dad. *Here we are!*

(*reads*)

Tweets: "Seaman made me feel unsafe in my own

country tonight, we are at risk." "Seaman will take women's rights back to the Stone Age." "Seaman's law is Sharia law with an American flag." "I'm eighteen and am scared for my life."

All written by young women. All written by young women who have mothers and fathers who care—at the end of the day—a lot more about their children than they do about putting you in office.

(*beat*)

Here's a good one. Look!

A cartoon of you on Fox, as a fox, coming out of a henhouse labeled Barnard with a pair of young hens in your mouth.

(*He crosses and she shows him the phone. He takes it from her. Meanwhile, ANSELM moves to AMIR.*)

ANSELM: Think about our current president, *how this man never takes the bait.* Be like him. Seaman is simply toying with you. You win by silence and compliance—anything else, you lose.

AMIR (*whispering loudly*): The SUIT!? What? Did you cast some crazy-ass kabbalistic Jewish *spell* on it to make him so impressive?

ANSELM: Remember what happened at Harvard? How it blew up your life and that of your parents when you let your feelings get in the way.

(SEAMAN *and* SRILANKA *have turned back into the room.*)

SEAMAN: Gentlemen. Srilanka seems to think that I
  should be less forceful in my language. My daughter
  believes I have crossed a line. With you. You have,
  I'll admit, agitated me. She would like me to be
  more conciliatory. Do you agree with her?

(AMIR *steels himself.*)

AMIR: I am just a tailor's apprentice. I beg your pardon
  if you took offense.
SEAMAN: Thank you, we put this behind us. Fresh
  starts. See, Srilanka?
SRILANKA: Dad, I'm afraid I have to abandon your
  debate prep tonight. Schuyler can do it. I have to go
  up to Barnard and apologize to the entire student
  body and explain that you are still unequivocal in
  your commitment to fairness for *all* women. I don't
  like what I'm seeing right now. You want to lead the
  world, well, act like a world leader, Dad.
SEAMAN (*weary*): Now, honey.

(*This is the last straw. She lights up. She confronts him.*)

SRILANKA: Don't you *dare*. "NOW, HONEY?" Not
  even for a second, ever, ever use that tone with me.
  I'm not some fucking *staffer* from *Wharton*. I'm not

some donor with a *request*! I'm not some minister from Moose Lake come to ask if you're *born again*!

I. Am. Not. To. Be. "Handled." You made me your campaign manager because you need one person to tell you the truth. Here's the truth, Father, you have become an unregulated force, careening between positions, wracked by a lack of sleep, and fueled by junk food and coffee, saying whatever comes into your head at any moment, and if you're not careful you won't just lose the race, *you'll lose everything*.

(*She goes to the elevator and pushes the button. PING. She looks at* AMIR. *The doors close.*)

SEAMAN (*troubled, weary*): This is very hard. This election. I, uh, I didn't realize, I thought at first, well, I'll make myself heard, I hate the people in politics, I thought the American people deserve so much more, a businessman. A businessman who has to deal with the realities and conditions on the ground, unions and contractors and merchants and deadlines and billing and overbilling and cheats, and I thought, "Who is gonna step in?" And I never knew how hard it would be.
(*beat*)
I don't think even my daughter understands this. Amir, do you think it's too much for her? Has she mentioned this?

AMIR: Ask me about fabrics and cuts of cloth. I only wish you to be happy in your purchase, sir.

SEAMAN: All I am doing is trying to get you to be who you really are, son, and not just a coward.

ANSELM: I am starting *not* to be comfortable, Mr. Seaman, with what is happening here.

SEAMAN (*cuts him off*): How will you realize your potential if you don't push back against *the Man*?

AMIR: *On the other hand* . . . Regarding your daughter—if you lack the capacity to discern right from wrong *yourself,* well, I think you should take her counsel very seriously. After all, a *moral compass* is useful only to *ordinary people,* those who have a quaint belief in the power of civility. Such a thing is not necessary for a *politician*; in fact, given your trajectory, it is quite clear that common decency is actually detrimental. So I would keep her around, as even sociopaths need canaries in their coal mines.

(*And the air is still.*)

SEAMAN: Didn't that feel good? Swinging at me? See—you can take me on!
(*beat*)
Okay. Huh, so I'm a sociopath and you're a Muslim with a low opinion of me. Hey, you just

went head-to-head with one of the most powerful men on the planet. And you did good. But. Listen.

(*beat*)

I learned something over the past year, I learned that what starts off as sort of an experiment, a "what-if," can turn real. "What if I ran for president so I became even more of a name?" "What if I said stuff nobody says but everybody thinks?" A lot of people say exactly what they think and end up losing everything. Not me. No. I say exactly what I think and suddenly it's true. Suddenly people want it, Amir. That's the story of America. That's the story so many foreigners don't get, that the line between lies and facts—actually there *is* no line, just a pulse beat.

(*beat*)

Think about my position on refugees. I mean, man, if you can't make it in your own country and you've got to flee—what kind of people are we taking in? They come to this country, and they don't have the resourcefulness to get what I got, and they invent their own persecution, because to put it like common folk, they're what I like to call "losers." A loser is someone who sabotages their own good luck. A loser is someone who has a cup full of luck and sees it half full with a giant leak in it. Are you a loser, Amir?

(*beat*)

    Well, are you?

AMIR (*quietly*): Perhaps you should subject me to one of
    your "loyalty oaths," sir, and find out.

SEAMAN: That might happen. See y'all in a week or so.

(*The elevator door PINGs and opens.* SEAMAN *gets in. Is
gone.*)

AMIR: This has become *way* dangerous. Get out of the
    deal, don't give him the suit, give him his filthy
    money back. Or I'm done, man, fuck all y'all. This is
    nuts.

ANSELM: Very, and very dangerous, yes, but actually,
    you're not quitting. Would you like to know
    why?

AMIR: Dude, *I don't care, man, blah blah blah, the
    better angels of his nature.* Oh, well. Yeah, *another*
    world I don't fit into.

    There's fucking politics here, too?

ANSELM: Where isn't there politics?

AMIR: I'm just gonna get on a bus and go to like Taos or
    somewhere burnouts go and make espressos for
    college kids and learn to ski. I give the fuck up on
    this life.

ANSELM: I think I know what happened here. He
    sensed—he knew—that you had emboldened his
    daughter to stand up to him.

AMIR: I didn't.

ANSELM (*ignores this lie*): He can't punish her. He needs her. But *you*—he can make you pay. Your pride. In engaging with him.

AMIR: He engaged me first.

ANSELM (*yelling*): *Stop lying to yourself* and *stop lying to me* and—

(*beat, calm*)

Look. We both know my eyes are failing and I can't do the close work without you. Okay? Let's admit it. And my hands? They shake and hurt. Are stiff. I don't know what it is. I'm afraid to find out.

(*beat*)

I can't finish the suit alone. You know that. Please stop pretending that you have not been fixing my errors for the past six months.

AMIR: Ten months.

ANSELM: Ten months. Thank you. So we have no choice, we're in a little battle for our lives, actually. And . . .

(*gently*)

You have now placed a target on your pious father, his undetermined citizenship. You think Kurt is dangerous to the nation? The world? He's dangerous to your world first.

(*beat*)

We withdraw the suit, and your parents are endangered. We finish the suit and your parents are safe.

(*beat*)

> Better, is it not, for them to be safe, to age quietly in Queens, near the mosque, near their friends, near me, who loves them and owes them so much—near their son, who is becoming wealthy enough to provide for them as they grow old and infirm. And who will have a wonderful thriving business because Anselm is retiring.

AMIR: You can't.

ANSELM: Let's face it, this fucker has killed me.

AMIR: We are trapped.

ANSELM: Yes. And I should not have accepted his custom, you were right, I was wrong, I apologize. Now. Let's get dinner?

(*beat*)

> A beer and some curry. It's fall in New York, Amir, the air is crisp, and perfect for walking, so all is not lost.

(*beat*)

> We must cherish small pleasures, you know; for in this day and age, they are often the greatest pleasures of all.

END OF ACT ONE, SCENE TWO

INTERMISSION

ACT TWO

(*A week later.* KURT SEAMAN *is in the atelier, in an armchair. A woman in her sixties, formidable, in conservative attire, a scarlet red suit, Senator* KITTY FINCH-GIBBON, *is standing. On the mannequin is the almost complete debate suit.*)

FINCH-GIBBON: I must say—an odd choice of places to meet.

SEAMAN: Why? Anselm is the soul of discretion. He made your suit, Senator Finch-Gibbon; he is making my suit; you asked for privacy and discretion. What more could the chair of the RNC want? Well, it's just us.

(*beat*)

That's a good suit. It's flattering—to your shape.

FINCH-GIBBON: Thank you, Kurt. You know, it's fine to call me Kitty. We've played badminton together.

SEAMAN: On my courts. I'm telling you, badminton is going to be very big, Seaman Badminton Team, paying for them to go to the Olympics! Have you seen those girls? It's like Amazonian-Sabra-Baywatch-Nymphet nirvana! I'd like to offer you honorary chair of the American Ladies League of Badminton.

Otherwise known as ALL BAD. In those little shorty-short skirts? Let's have a drink, Kit, it's five; scotch?

FINCH-GIBBON: Vodka.

SEAMAN: Neat?

FINCH-GIBBON: Rocks.

(*He pours them a drink.*)

SEAMAN: What do you think of mine?

(*Points to the mannequin*)

The suit. For the debate.

FINCH-GIBBON: Yes, Anselm makes the best suits. He did a suit for my late husband's open casket.

SEAMAN: He was a great astronaut, your late husband,

yep, Butch Finch, too bad the rocket was a dud.
Didn't even get off the ground, they just were
electrocuted by crappy workmanship, and that's
what I'm gonna change. Probably if I investigated
we'd find the rocket was built by illegal South
American aliens.

FINCH-GIBBON: There was an investigation. It was
nothing of the sort—there was a short in the
alternator!

SEAMAN (*laughing*): Oh, who knows, we don't know for
sure! Exciting times, really, and I have to say, the
party, they were balky at first. You were. But you all
came around because everyone needs a win, and
here we are, aren't we.

(*He clinks glasses*)

So, are we here to discuss money? Let's just get right
to it.

FINCH-GIBBON: Kurt, it's a very large figure.

SEAMAN: "Large" is my second-favorite word
except when it comes to women's hips and
waiters' tips.

FINCH-GIBBON: You can drop the fake crassness,
actually. That would be a relief. For the sake of both
of our stomachs. How about that?

SEAMAN: I'm not being crass, Kitty.

(*suddenly all ice*)

I'm just talking to you with the respect I think you
deserve.

FINCH-GIBBON: As long as we're being clear about our terms, Kurt. We've tried to be cooperative.

(*There is a PING.* SRILANKA *enters, wearing a gray flannel suit. The outfit imagined by* AMIR *for her.* AMIR *enters the room behind her.*)

SEAMAN: Ah. Well. Look who's here. Darling, you've met Senator Kitty Finch-Gibbon, haven't you?

FINCH-GIBBON: Yes. And how wonderful that you've taken such an active role in your father's campaign.

SRILANKA: Thank you. A steep learning curve.

FINCH-GIBBON: You could do this for a living if you liked, my dear.

(*beat, to* SEAMAN)

You've had a rough few weeks, Kurt. Many people attribute your uptick in the polls to your daughter's iron fist.

SRILANKA (*cheerful*): Yes, I certainly laid down the law.

FINCH-GIBBON: After the infamous Barnard/Fox flip-flop fiasco.

SEAMAN: Will you look at that suit?

SRILANKA: Yes. Amir made it. Can we speak alone, Dad, for a moment?

SEAMAN: You made it? Amir? Did you? Wow. It's fantastic.

FINCH-GIBBON (*to* AMIR): It's very lovely. I wonder if I may commission something similar but in grape?

[62]

AMIR: Sir—I need to ask you something. My father, his hot dog carts. He is being harassed. Green card issues. License questions. Spot health inspections, since last week. I wonder if you might know anything about this?

SEAMAN (*looks at his daughter*): Amir. I have a lot on my plate. So, no. Nor am I that petty. I do not harass *hot dog cart people*.

AMIR: Please, please, if you are, just . . . stop, they're old, they're struggling . . . I am imploring you—

SEAMAN: Son. Son. Hey. You have my word. If your parents are kosher, you have my word.

AMIR: If they're—

SEAMAN (*very warm and gracious*): I know I was not my best self last time we talked, and I don't sleep enough and I am a little on edge, you know, running for president and stuff. But I really did put it all behind me, haven't thought about it, and listen, you gave as good as you got and—

(*regarding* SRILANKA's *suit*)

My God, you are skilled. But I don't think you're needed any longer, Amir. This is a private meeting.

(*A beat.* AMIR *catches* SRILANKA's *eye. He leaves. A moment.*)

SRILANKA (*after he's gone*): That is *exactly* who you harass. You have made me a promise. There will be *no lies. Not to me.*

SEAMAN: And I am not. The charge is not even worth dignifying. Honey. Please. Kitty, let's proceed.

FINCH-GIBBON: Please, Srilanka, would you sit down. I would like your counsel as Kurt's campaign manager and daughter.

(SRILANKA *sits.*)

I am not here, strictly speaking, in my official capacity as the party chairwoman. Rather, I am here representing a number of political and business leaders from both sides of the aisle who are very worried, and who feel that the only solution is to offer you a large figure. In order to protect the country and our interests.

SEAMAN: It's what I've been saying, it costs money, it costs money not to be a loser.

FINCH-GIBBON: We would like you to be a loser.

SEAMAN: What?

FINCH-GIBBON: Lose. We don't feel that you are the person to take us where we need to go. The College Republicans of America are about to denounce you.

SEAMAN: Oh, come on, *college Republicans*? That's what you've got? They're whining self-congratulatory little preppy pricks who never worked for anything in their spoiled little lives—

FINCH-GIBBON: I think you may have mistaken this visit for a discussion; please, rest assured, it is not.

SEAMAN (*over her*): What do the kids at Texas Poly say! What do the kids at the Colorado School of Mines say, what do the workers in Texarkana say! *They* matter! Look, after Barnard, I lost some women, but what I *got* was every unemployed blue-collar worker from Maine to Monterey.

FINCH-GIBBON: Nevertheless.

SEAMAN: Nevertheless?

FINCH-GIBBON: There is a sense that you are ill. We have had several forensic psychiatrists analyze you, and the findings are all quite similar and striking and, dare I say, blood-chilling. We feel certain that the military will not take orders from a man they consider to be unhinged. The people who work at the Defense Department and in the offices of the Joint Chiefs of Staff are the longest-serving and most sober public servants this nation has. They have let it be known that you present certain very knotty obstacles to the chain of command in that you are generally speaking considered stark raving mad.

SEAMAN (*amused*): Not.

FINCH-GIBBON: These parties are deeply disinvested in having a trade war with China for you, or any other kind of war for you. North Korea is your biggest fan and they have through the Dark Web secretly been your biggest donor. We have proof.

SEAMAN: Please, proof is so subjective.

FINCH-GIBBON: The chairman of the Fed and the heads of five banks are concerned that your presidency will result in a Great Depression that will make 1929 seem like a minor market downturn.

Many of the members of the party who have endorsed you have done so simply because they are chickenshit little candy-ass cowards with their bloomers over their waists and you actually have made threats to them. The people who have charged me with seeing you today are impervious to threats.

SEAMAN: Who? What people? Who could you be talking about, Kitters?

SRILANKA: Dad. Just let her finish. Please.

(*to* FINCH-GIBBON)

And how do you suggest this happen?

FINCH-GIBBON: We would propose that your father withdraw from the race on grounds of illness.

SEAMAN (*entertained*): What illness? Is my poor little heart too fragile to take the stress?

(*roaring*)

Do I have *the vapors*? *Syphilis!*

FINCH-GIBBON: We will make you entirely whole. You have never had as much money as you claim, and we are, between us, this group, able to offer you two billion dollars not to become the next president. The terms can be negotiated, of course. You could claim the victory of having run. But it has been decided that the cynicism you have engendered, the anger you have stirred up in the voting public, is not desirable.

SEAMAN: You think I could win this thing.

FINCH-GIBBON: After careful consideration, I would say . . . that is a chance that we are unwilling to take.

SEAMAN: Hear that, Srilanka, the cabal has come up with a cool two and *a half* billion bucks for me to take a fall. Isn't that something. How'd you come up with that figure?

FINCH-GIBBON: It is a figure agreed upon by actuaries, by certain national security experts, and a thinking working group made up of three ministers from the Anglican Church, four Episcopalian leaders, one Jesuit, two rabbis, people from SAG and AFTRA, and a few very, very, very concerned citizens of means. I am their representative. We met in Aspen on several occasions during the campaign with growing dismay.

SEAMAN: *Love* Aspen. But that ain't a figure that makes my heart leap. Srilanka here, she would be incredibly offended by the idea of me taking— let's face it—a bribe, really. She wouldn't be able to look me in the eye ever again.

SRILANKA: Stop, please, Dad. Listen to her offer.

SEAMAN: She's everything to me. She was a little girl,

we were standing on the beach in Southampton or maybe it was Bermuda, and she said, "Daddy, you can be president someday, you'd be the best president *ever*." And I told her I would do it for her. For my little girl. Didn't I, my dear?

SRILANKA: *Take it, Dad. Please.* Take it.

SEAMAN (*astonished*): Take it? *Take it?*

SRILANKA: Yes. Before this gets worse.

SEAMAN: *Worse?* Things are *terrific*! Some people want me to be president and some *other* assholes want to bribe me not to be, it's the deal of the century, it's like win-win-win.

SRILANKA: I don't think you should be cavalier—

SEAMAN: I promised you I'd be the president.

SRILANKA: I was eight. *I was eight years old!*

SEAMAN (*affronted*): You know how important my *word* is. Have I ever promised you anything and not delivered? You were eight and wanted an animatronic cat and I had one made! In Korea. When your beloved little rat terrier Tippi Hedren died I had her cloned. *In Korea.* Have you learned nothing from me about negotiating, sweetheart? Just watch and listen.

(*to* KITTY, *engaged*)

First of all, I gotta say it's an insulting offer, not just to me, but to the millions of people who have gotten behind me, this group of people who are part of a revolution of the American soul.

FINCH-GIBBON: Mr. Seaman. It is precisely the excitement of those many people we are attempting to preserve. You are a wonderful pitchman, but your follow-through is virtually nil. It is the follow-through of a water spaniel.

SEAMAN: Those dogs are fabulous!

SRILANKA: Dad, what is it that you want?

SEAMAN: An opportunity, when it's a good opportunity, does not merely have one positive outcome, you know this, my dear, I've taught you this. It has several possible, even mutually *exclusive* and contradictory, wonderful outcomes. An opportunity should land like a star on the American flag, with many points to it. Or like a cluster bomb, exploding in multiple places! That is the art of deal making.

SRILANKA (*alarmed recognition*): So wait. Did you plan to buy and sell the presidency of the United States of America all along?

FINCH-GIBBON: We think he might have had this in mind all along, didn't you, Kurt? The truth is, you don't want the job. Aside from the plane, it's not very much fun. It's very restrictive. The qualities you value—improvisation, spontaneity, caprice and impulse, whimsy and vengeance—they will not serve you well. It requires steadiness.

SEAMAN (*delighted, laughs*): Ooooh, I don't think that's in the job description, honey.

FINCH-GIBBON: It is a game of chess and you must be
    able to think many moves ahead—when we have
    had presidents that lacked that fundamental skill,
    chaos ensued. You are unpredictable. And in
    politics, given the state of the world today, being
    unpredictable is deadly. I say this as someone who
    spent many years on the House Intelligence
    Committee and as the ex-ambassador to
    Montenegro.
(*beat; ice and steel*)
    On a personal note, let me say this: you and your
    frivolous campaign, one fueled by the *capriciousness*
    deep within your dark, decaying, and *very shallow
    husk* of a soul—*have simply broken my heart.*
(*beat*)
    Broken my heart. You are not a conservative. You
    do not value hard work, and caution to social
    change.
        Conservatives respect tradition; not shortcuts
    and recurrent bankruptcies. Not recklessness of
    deed and impulse, not casual epithets and
    vocabularies limited to "loser," "best," "pussy," and
    the almost hallucinatory use of the word "I."
SEAMAN: You have no idea what you are talking about.
FINCH-GIBBON: And in leading by example. *You*, Kurt,
    are simply a carny freak. The *single* principle by
    which you operate seems to be irreducible

self-interest. I endured the anti-intellectualism and extremism of the Tea Party, and even sympathized with their anger; I gritted my teeth at the deniers of science and the fringe religious zealots who envisioned Jesus Christ swooping down upon the back of a pterodactyl. *But you, sir,* I have never seen anything like you in fifty years of public service stretching from the Nebraska School Board, and then State House, to chair of our party. You have vaporized the qualities that make conservativeness vital to a society. By bullying and demeaning and vomiting invective and insinuations, you have given birth to a pitchfork-bearing brigade of carnivorous cannibals. My colleagues may think you are simply ill. I, however, maintain that you are not even human but an entity, a demon Manchurian Candidate sent by Beelzebub, for all I know, to herald the breaking of some Seventh Seal. If you are indeed simply mentally diminished—then what you have done to our party will take generations to undo. And when I'm done with you, I'm gonna go after the cowards who made you possible. I am brokenhearted, and had to take anti-nausea medication and a suppository simply to be in your presence.

SEAMAN (*cuts her off, yells*): BELTWAY!

FINCH-GIBBON (*nonplussed*): Huh?

SEAMAN: *Beltway! Beltway!*

FINCH-GIBBON: *What?*

SEAMAN: Shut up, *please. God.* You pious hypocrites and your Beltway bullshit. *Please would you shut up and just tell me how much it's worth for me to do this thing.* The figure I mentioned. *If you doubled it.* If you doubled it. We could talk.

FINCH-GIBBON (*astonished*): Five billion. You are asking for five billion dollars to go away.

SEAMAN (*carefully saying each word*): Five. Billion. Bouncing. Bucks. Go check with your bosses, whoever they are. I don't like having Gates close on me or being Buffetted, or Blankly Fined. It's so Bush league.

FINCH-GIBBON: Cute, Kurt. Very cute.

(*on the phone*)

It's me . . .

(*She walks away, talking on the phone.*)

SEAMAN (*to* SRILANKA): Doesn't that have terrific alliteration, my darling! "Five billion bouncing bucks left the buckets of the elitist cabal and crept into Kurt's Cayman Islands bank account!" I like the sound of that.

FINCH-GIBBON (*on the phone*): I know it's more than we agreed on, Hiram, but—

SEAMAN (*to* FINCH-GIBBON): Don't think too long, dearie.

FINCH-GIBBON (*on phone*): Well, I mean, I don't think
he's going to budge, I don't think I *can* get him
lower.

(*furious*)

What if we threw in those Arabian stallions you
own, Lewis!

(*beat*)

Listen, I liquidated seventeen acres of Palm Beach
beachfront to go in on this, you can sell your
fucking horses!

(*beat, contempt*)

Oh well, sell some of those Haliburton shares,
Charlene, *please*.

SEAMAN: You gotta love this, right, honey, this is maybe
the best day of business ever for me. Too bad I won't
be able to write about it. Of course, I probably won't
take it.

SRILANKA: Take it. I absolve you of the farce of a
promise made to an eight-year-old on a beach. This
is a much better proposition. You can honorably
walk away.

SEAMAN: No. It would crush me if you were to stop
believing in me. Srilanka, whatever I am doing, it is
for the family. Family comes before everything. And
your fiancé is worried about you. Schuyler is worried.
He tells me there's been a lack of intimacy. For
weeks now . . .

(SRILANKA *stares at him, deciding what to say.*)

FINCH-GIBBON (*on phone*): Don't you *dare* tell me to
　　sell the Constable, David, unless you're prepared to
　　sell that hideous Jasper Johns thing you have over
　　your staircase in Beverly Hills!
(*beat, sarcastic*)
　　Oh, *Rauschenberg*, sorry!
SRILANKA (*calmly direct*): Well, frankly, Dad, I'm not
　　entirely sure that Schuyler loves *me*, but more to the
　　point, I think you don't realize that *you're* actually
　　starting to damage the family.
SEAMAN: No.
SRILANKA: When you began this campaign, I
　　believed it was for the right reasons. But at a
　　certain point, you started to change. It was no
　　longer about the economy, and kicking out the
　　calcified old guard, but suddenly you became
　　fixated on *enemies*.
SEAMAN: But Sri-Sri—*enemies* are far more important
　　than friends; your *friends* you can *always* ignore,
　　but *enemies* require *constant* attention and can
　　never be taken for granted.
SRILANKA: So it's family first, then enemies, and then
　　your friends?
FINCH-GIBBON (*on phone*): This will be over soon,
　　Lewis, if we throw in the horse. Thanks, yes, it *is*
　　better than killing him.

(*She hangs up. The elevator PINGs and* AMIR *and* ANSELM *disembark into the room.* AMIR *is holding a woman's suit, for* KITTY FINCH-GIBBON.)

ANSELM (*to* FINCH-GIBBON): Here it is, your suit with which to launch the USS *Custer.*
(*to* SEAMAN *and* SRILANKA)
    I'm so thrilled you could use my place of work as a discreet room for a meeting.
SEAMAN (*dry*): Yeah, so am I.
ANSELM: Henry Kissinger tried to persuade Kirk Douglas to play him in a bio-pic right where we are standing. I put them together.
    They could not reach terms. It would have been a wonderful film. My first credit as a producer; alas, that film was not ever to be—though I am an associate producer on a movie called *Bugzilla*, because the producer owed me for three cashmere sports coats—

(FINCH-GIBBON *stares at* SEAMAN.)

SEAMAN: Go on, Kitty. We are among friends.
FINCH-GIBBON: We are prepared to go to three-seven. Three point seven billion dollars plus a very good Constable painting.
(*beat, attempting dignity*)
    And a priceless Robert Rauschenberg. And an Arabian stallion named Sir Kicks-a-Lot.

[75]

SEAMAN (*scoffs*): *Sir Kicks-a-Lot?* Everyone knows that horse is a lox. He can't screw worth a damn anymore. No. I refuse to even discuss that ridiculous offer. Be gone with that. Anselm, Amir, the suit looks gorgeous. Let's try it. Let's try it on.

ANSELM (as AMIR *readies the suit*): It's not entirely done, but it's close. After this fitting it will be ready. Some stitching to finalize is all that remains.

AMIR: The buttons. You'll love 'em. They're gold, from a very small mine in Zimbabwe.

SEAMAN: Zimbabwe. We have a resort there for big-game hunters.

(*gently*)

The suit you made for my daughter is *stunning*. You're very skilled. More than I even knew! Made lovingly, and with such attention to detailed measurements. The fit!

SRILANKA: A gift.

SEAMAN (*to* AMIR): Gift! Generous. I think it's great that you had time for fittings.

(*to* ANSELM)

The apprentice has perhaps caught up with the master, maybe?

AMIR: I will never have the skill and grace of my mentor.

ANSELM: Senator Finch-Gibbon, would you like to try yours on, please? I do need to see it to make sure it's exactly right.

FINCH-GIBBON: Anselm, I don't think this is exactly the right moment—

SEAMAN (*over her*): Oh, go on. Kill two birds with one stone; a suit and a presidency. Go on, Kitty, try on your "Good Ship Lollipop" look. You don't wanna launch a coup in an ill-fitting suit, *bube*.

(*She takes her suit and reluctantly goes behind the curtain of the dressing room.*)

ANSELM: Mr. Seaman. Try on the suit, please.

(SEAMAN *takes the suit from* AMIR *and goes behind the curtain of the other dressing room.*)

SEAMAN (*through the curtain*): Now, Kitty—the three-seven, you're headed in the right direction, you're getting *warmer*, but we're still not there. It's still not in the realm of the entertainable. *Oh, wow.*

This is *something else, boys.*

You have really done it. *Wow.* Kitty, I hope yours is as good as mine, I hope it's as good for you as this one is for me! Kitty, what you fail to understand, when you complain about how unpredictable I am, and so on, the people you're talking for, well, really, I am not going to be your president. Oh, yes. I'll buy you, I'll make sure you get *blamed* when shit goes wrong, but I'm not *yours*. How could you think that? No. I'm for *the Others*.

(*beat*)

Ladies and gentlemen, the suit.

(*He emerges. He looks wonderful. He looks statesman-like.* FINCH-GIBBON *emerges as well, in her nautical-blue pantsuit with epaulets and frogging and even a captain's cap. They stare at each other.*)

FINCH-GIBBON: I can go to four. There are limits.

SEAMAN: You look good; you look like you're in a musical, Kitty.

ANSELM (*weakly*): You look wonderful, Senator. As do you, Mr. Seaman.

SEAMAN: Thanks, Anselm.

(*back to* FINCH-GIBBON)

Four? Kitty cat, please try and understand: the Americans I speak to, these Others, they live in a very dangerous world. My Americans—the Others—are broken and sick of being lied to and screwed over, they have nothing. They cannot even begin to tabulate the list of betrayals perpetrated on them.

(*beat*)

Perpetrated on them by *who*? Not *me*.

FINCH-GIBBON: Four-two.

SEAMAN: Let me tell you something, I met this old lady,

Maggie Dodelson, she looked seventy, was probably thirty-nine or so, in Coleslaw, Ohio, you know, campaign stop, she worked at a frozen chocolate banana joint called Choc-Nana's Choc-Nutty Emporium, in a mall, which was mostly abandoned. Divorced, two kids, and her wages had stagnated and she needed food stamps to just feed her boys, Chip and Kip. Who were living virtually on a diet of Choc-Nana rejects and broken bits. She had lumbago and rickets and her property taxes kept going up and up, and everyone else got a bailout, big banks, big shots, auto manufacturers, given to them by—well, now—who, Kitty? Could it have been *you*, Kitty? Had *you* voted for those things? YES!

(*lethal, very dangerous*)

And Maggie Dodelson, she got *nothing*. She got bubkes, she got shafted. And she came to my rally, and made her way up to me and said, "Listen, the American dream, it left me in the dust a long, *long* time ago, Kurt. This American-experiment bullshit is over. Take the fuckers down, Kurt. Take them all down. A vote for Kurt Seaman is a vote to take the whole motherfucking thing down."

(*beat, deadly*)

And that seems like a nice idea.

FINCH-GIBBON: Four billion, four hundred twenty million.

SEAMAN: I don't think—why is this so very hard for you to understand? No. To walk away from Maggie Dodelson at this point when she needs me the most, it's five billion. Take it or leave it. Five.

(*to* ANSELM *and* AMIR)

Anselm, Amir, kids—make whatever adjustments you need to. It's fantastic, it's a killer suit.

(*turns to* FINCH-GIBBON, *ice*)

Absolutely killer.

(*beat*)

Well. I'm going to be late. I've gotta fly to Scranton for the opening of my condos there, Seaman Fountains.

(*beat*)

Anselm, you're done? Good. Kitty dear, what's your answer?

FINCH-GIBBON: You will blow the debate so badly that even your most fervent acolyte cannot help but be repulsed.

SEAMAN (*chuckling*): That's gonna take a lot.

FINCH-GIBBON: Don't fuck with us, Kurt. My people, don't forget who we are, we beat the redcoats. We gave the Indians smallpox. My people, we dropped two nuclear bombs. And we invented white bread.

SEAMAN: That's great, my dear. But what have you done lately? Except bail out banks and cars and lose every war you got us into.

FINCH-GIBBON: You get your five billion.

(*He goes back into the dressing room.* KITTY FINCH-GIBBON *goes to the drinks cart as though dazed, and pours herself a long vodka.*)

SEAMAN (*behind the curtain*): Better figure out some
    way to park the cash for me, some down payment
    show of good faith, say, half of the total, somewhere
    smart that you kids have access to. Say a little bank
    in Panama that can't be hacked. Oh, and I also
    want the horsey and the pictures.
FINCH-GIBBON: You are doing the right thing. And
    those who know will always consider you a great
    American patriot—and a selfless man.

(*She walks to the elevator and hits the button. PING.*)

ANSELM: Senator, you left your clothes—do you—
FINCH-GIBBON: Burn them. Burn them, please.

(*The doors close and she is gone.* SEAMAN *emerges from
the dressing room in his prior outfit.*)

SEAMAN (*dead serious*): What happened here today,
    what you were witness to, that is strictly private,
    of course.

ANSELM: That goes without saying.

SEAMAN: To you, maybe, but what about to your young genius here. Does he know what a confidentiality agreement is?

AMIR: Mr. Seaman. And I never signed such a—

SRILANKA (*cuts him off*): If Anselm did, legally it applies to you as well. I'm sorry. It's a fact. Amir. Please. Listen to me. There are windmills to tilt at but this one has razors on it.

(AMIR *looks at* SEAMAN.)

AMIR: But. You just conned the American people out of an honest election for five billion dollars. People should know—

SEAMAN (*kindly, cunning*): Conned? Son, I didn't con anyone.

AMIR: What was I just witness to, then?

SEAMAN: I don't know what you *think* you saw, but there was nothing untoward about it.

AMIR: No, this wasn't a deal to sell the presidency?

SEAMAN: Of course not. What you were privy to may have been a discussion about my future role in the business of America. How I could best serve my country. *Now*, I might or might not have begun to discuss a business arrangement with some private *citizens* with *far too much* time and money on their hands. I may have taken steps to liberate them of some of their grotesque ill-gotten insider-traded gains, but I did not in any way, shape, or form *con anyone*. And to suggest so is libelous. Libel is ugly. Slander. Ugly.

(*beat*)

And frankly, I'd like to help you. I see so much in you. I'd like to offer you a deal.

AMIR: Would you? Please. This should be good.

SEAMAN: You're just about done with your apprenticeship, Anselm has taught you so much. My God, that suit for Srilanka is as good as mine, and I certainly think it has some potent magic to it, because she is very much entranced by *you*. Isn't she?

(*beat*)

Look at her! It is perfect, it shows off her beautiful silhouette so artfully. It must have taken a lot of very close measuring. *Lot of touching.*

(*beat*)

So. Come work for me, design your own line of very high-end suits. Of course, your pay package would start in the high upper mid six figures. And a five-year contract. There'd be a lot of travel. Lot of time in London. Asia. And our headquarters in Abu Dhabi—would be your home base.

AMIR: I somehow have a feeling that this is not an offer, exactly, but rather a carrot that is attached to a stick.

SEAMAN: I want this boy to do well. To triumph against

the forces pulling at him. A *father* whose immigration status is *shaky*.

A *father* who worships at the mosque in Queens, Abu Al Mahir, that has been host to some very unsavory extremists. A *father* who is part of a study group at this mosque, some of whose members of this study group have studied new techniques in homemade things that go BOOM. And as for *you*, a young man who threw away the generosity of so many who believed in him, who used his education, paid for by *others*, to become a violent anti-American infiltrator of Harvard, and who spilled goat blood on *our flag* and burned it, in the most overt act of ingratitude I can think of—I want you to accept that even with all these terrible black marks, you can *still* succeed in America. If you accept America.

(*beat*)

And of course, you know, don't make any more clothing for Srilanka, kinda.

AMIR: Please explain to me that this is not an actual threat.

SRILANKA: I know what this is really about.

(*turns to her father*)

Your anger at Amir is misdirected. Don't take your anger at me out on him.

SEAMAN: I am not angry, honey, I would be if you

weren't my child but—you need to come back down to earth. This campaign has sort of driven all of us to extremes. And it's time to go back to basics. Like Schuyler. And giving me grandchildren.

Continuing this family.

SRILANKA: Do you think that something happened between Amir and me?

AMIR: I actually feel slightly bad for you, Mr. Seaman.

SEAMAN: Would that not be the ultimate win for you? Desecrating my precious daughter?

SRILANKA: My God. Do you hear yourself— desecrating? Is that how you see me?

SEAMAN: His greatest win. To *get* to my daughter, in body or in mind.

(AMIR *finally laughs.*)

AMIR: You poor, poor, pathetic fucker.

SRILANKA: Amir. Please don't—

AMIR (*ignores her; at* SEAMAN): Unlike you, winning is simply not one of those things I think about, actually. It's not much on my radar. I know that makes me disgusting to you, sort of faggy, isn't it, to you, but I've always found that people who are obsessed with winning are quite often, *let's face it,* almost hallucinatory in their dullness. "Win." The ultimate win. How dull. How boring.

Winning! Yeah, like that poor actor,
"Winnnnning."

(*quietly*)

How can a man as weak as you ever know what it
feels like to win? You are a failure in the deepest
part of yourself, with your affairs, your terror and
loathing of women, your limited curiosity, your
stunted maturity; why, *you can never win, Kurt.*
You wouldn't know what it *felt* like if you did.
Because you have a secret hiding in plain sight; you
have only the most limited experience of love. Even
for your children, your daughter, you love them as
reflections of what you have. Me? I have a family I
love—a real father who loves America more than
you could ever imagine. And this man who has
been a real mentor, a real one, not like you and your
bullying sideshow. Winning?

SRILANKA: Please stop.

AMIR (*to* SRILANKA, *utterly flat*): I'm sorry. I can't. I
can't stop it.

(*to* SEAMAN)

Your failure will destroy you finally, as the country
sinks into your reality and sees how they have been
betrayed by a tiny little man. They will only awaken
when America becomes a failing corporation to be
absorbed and stripped and sold for parts. To your
own pals. My God, what will you do when you have

nobody left to play with except other con artists and bullies and cheats who have duped the masses in America?

All those long nights while American cities burn because of you, and you realize that the Chinese and the Russians and even—oh my God—the Mexicans were so much smarter than you. You do not know history. I actually do.

(*beat*)

So. What will you do at two in the morning when leaders abroad and at home are planning how next to humiliate this once-great country. What will you do when the thugs you inspired run out of people to beat, and turn on one another, and then, of course, on you, Kurt, and your beloved family?

Will you feel like a winner then? *Another win! Another win!*

(*beat*)

I curse you to win, I pray you do.

I will watch, I will go back to being a man who reads newspapers and watches the news, just so that the movie of you, like some anemic Icarus always falling, will never fucking end.

(SEAMAN *looks stunned*)

Another hollow win for Kurt Seaman. Look at your future, look at what you've conjured for yourself. *You are doomed.*

SRILANKA: That's enough.

AMIR: You tell yourself you did this for your family, for your daughter, for your grandchildren, but you'll realize that is a lie when you look into your daughter's eyes and see what's really there. You love nobody but yourself, and you don't even know how to do that very well. I'm just telling you facts here.

You've already crossed your Rubicon. You've already given the ferryman your coin. It's already written. Look into your daughter's eyes. See the future. Everything I just said is in her eyes. It's all true. Look at her.

(*beat, intensely intimate*)

Srilanka, your father is simply insane. And insane people cannot help themselves. I know this, because of course, I am insane, too.

(*He takes the elevator. PING.* AMIR *is gone. Silence.*)

SEAMAN (*quietly, shaking*): That will not stand. What he did.

(*bewildered*)

What did he do? What he did? It will not stand.

(*a whisper*)

Did he put a curse on—I'll tell everyone, I know what he is, what his father is, what they are, evil subversives, and you? Anselm—to have given these demons sustenance for all these years—who really are you? Yeah, you say you're a Jewish Arab, but that—what does that even mean? Are you one of them?

ANSELM: I am just a maker of suits, a tailor, who committed to making you the greatest suit of all time, is who I am. And here it is. I did it. I have done it. It is almost yours. But not quite.

(*beat*)

My people have a story, of the Golem, a monster made of mud. He was conjured up by a holy man to do his bidding, to serve him. He was imbued with a force not of this world, but of another. Sometimes when I make a particular suit, I meditate upon the Golem. And I did so with your suit. It does have power. You felt it.

But, if anything happens to Amir, or to his family, *it will not serve you*. I made it. The suit will know.

SEAMAN: The only Golem in this room is me.

SRILANKA: Dad, it's a terrible thing to love someone too much. To love someone to the exclusion of reality, to the point where you are blind. Blind to the sum of their worst parts.

(*Shakes her head*)

I have never tested your love, but I am testing it now. I need you to look at me and tell me that you actually know I love you too much and that you are sorry. Sorry for the bullying you have embraced here. Sorry for what you've allowed *us* to become. If you can do that, and say "I'm sorry," this might heal, in time.

(*He does not look. He pushes the elevator button. PING! He enters, with his back to her.*)

SEAMAN: That five billion is gonna look pretty good to you and Schuyler and the kiddies, when this country blows up and you need a stateroom on the ark.

(*Elevator closes. He is gone.*)

ANSELM (*to* SRILANKA): Srilanka, I am sorry. I'll bring the suit to Seaman Towers myself, tomorrow, in time for the debate. This is going to take a great deal of work to finish.

END OF ACT TWO, SCENE ONE

(*In the dark we hear a voice. That of a woman anchor. Lights come up. Downstage is* KURT SEAMAN *in a spotlight, sitting on a stool. It is the debate.*)

(*Upstage, in the atelier, in very dim light,* ANSELM, AMIR, *and* SRILANKA *are watching on a laptop. The glow of the computer flickers about their faces. They all have drinks. They look worried.*)

MODERATOR (*over loudspeaker*): You have five minutes to answer, Mr. Seaman.

AMIR: He's doing too well.

SRILANKA: He's up to something?

ANSELM: Watch—shhhush . . .

SEAMAN: That's a great question, Elinor, really super
question, if not *the* question. Safety. Security and
the American dream. In the twenty-first century.

(*beat*)

But first, I've got to address something. The
"chatter" by the corrupt mainstream media. Listen:
My daughter has not withdrawn as campaign
manager. She is just taking a moment to be with her
fiancé—to be home. There is no tighter bond than
the one between my daughter and myself. So let's
put that to bed.

SRILANKA: He's lying. I quit the campaign this
morning.

SEAMAN: *Now.* Let's talk about the toxic trio of threats
to America. Number one—Islamic terrorists.
Number two—countries like China, Iran, and
North Korea. *And finally,* the most dangerous one
of all—the one *from within.* We have reached a
tipping point, America! Right? I meet people afraid
to go to the malls, to the movies, to train stations.
But with me, you will not be afraid anymore.

(*beat*)

Because—let's face it!—I am the only person on
this stage here at gorgeous Baylor University who

knows about the real, the real ugliness of having enemies. Because, listen. I've had enemies all my life.

(*intense*)

But—I've never lost a fight. Think about *that*. I have never lost a *single fight in my entire life*. And that's who you want to protect you.

(*a philosophical shrug*)

Maybe it's cost me something in polite society.

But . . . Hey. "They" keep waiting for me to stumble.

(*a laugh of incredulity*)

Look at what "they've" thrown at me now! My contempt for women. Please, every woman I've ever *known* will tell you that I love women more than I love creating wealth. And we know how much I love *that*.

(*smiles, thinks*)

"They" have a special army called the "Language Police." Yeah. The Language Police! They have commodified *hysteria*, and turned it into their currency. They have *criminalized* a sense of humor, and are attempting what I call "The Great National Vasectomy."

(*to the camera, ice*)

So. Are you watching me, Liberal America? Are you listening?

(*beat*)

I. Can. Not. Be. Stopped. And your time is coming
to an end! Your victim's rights and coddling and
everyone getting a prize for just showing up—

(*roaring*)

That is not the America that Lewis and Clark went
in search of! That is not the America that Moses
foretold and that God gave us! You must choose
who you want for your president as America teeters
over the great chasm of fire. When I'm done I will
have testified from the mountaintop. Because we
have reached a turning point! I want to talk to the
real America tonight! Tonight we name names!
And can you please shut that baby up!

(SEAMAN *composes himself.*)

ANSELM: Srilanka, what is he doing?

AMIR: He is supposed to be throwing the debate.

SRILANKA: He's calculating.

AMIR (*finishing for her*): He's winning. Is what he's
doing—did you give him those lines about
"Language Police"?

SRILANKA: Weeks ago. He is up to something big.

AMIR: Yeah, five billion dollars big.

ANSELM: He will not win this debate. Trust me.

SEAMAN: *Here* is the *ultimate* truth. The terrifying
truth. *Guess. Who's. Watching?* In the Middle East in

mosques and minarets, glued to their screens, trying to calculate the chances of us halting the plague of Islamic radicals. Named it! In North Korea, the Great Leader for Life trying to figure out whether we elect Ms. Pantsuit or *me*, who will push the button that simply makes them vanish into oblivion. Named that one, too!

Kim—finger. Button. Try me. See—I have something my opponent can never have, my friends: I HAVE BALLS!

MODERATOR: Mr. Seaman, you're over your time limit—

SEAMAN (*roaring, cuts her off*): *I am not* over but *she* is! Let's face it! Who are the most dangerous enemies of all? The ones in our own homes. Let's name them!

(*quietly, fear-inducing*)

There's an entire liberal segment of society watching this debate with bated breath; in New York, LA, Chicago—the ones who would open borders because they are moved by words rusting on the Statue of Liberty: Take in "the wretched refuse of your teeming shore, I lift my lamp beside the golden door!"

(*beat*)

Guess what, folks: I do not lift my lamp beside the golden door, I nail it shut because nowadays the

"wretched refuse of your teeming shore" have
bombs strapped to their chests!

(*It is at this moment that both of the arms fall off the suit
jacket worn by* SEAMAN. *He looks down.*)

AMIR: Anselm, you're a magician!

ANSELM: Quiet! Watch!

SEAMAN (*catching his breath*): Oh man, oops. Wow.
    Boy. That's good. Quality ain't what it used to be.
    You wouldn't believe what I paid for this thing, but
    there'll be a response from me—yeah—you don't
    screw Kurt Seaman.

(*beat*)

    Where was I? Enemies. I'll tell you a little story
    about enemies at home. There is a little man. A little
    man in Brooklyn. A little Muslim man with some
    hot dog carts, one outside Seaman Tower on Fifth,
    others in Central Park, a nice, unassuming little
    man who worships at a mosque in Queens, Abu Al
    Mahir, where a number of people are recruited to
    go overseas and become jihadist killers, and he is
    part of the study group from which those boys were
    recruited, and his name is Manouchehr Masoud
    and you may have bought an all-American hot dog
    from him without knowing it. And he has a son.
    Amir Masoud. He was given all the opportunities

and scholarships available to a bright young
minority person, the son of Islamic immigrants!
And what did he do with his scholarship to Harvard?
(*violent astonishment*)
He burned an American flag on the Yard! He
defiled the flag! Arrest these people and send them
to the darkest, iciest frozen jail where the sun never
shines—
AMIR: Oh my God! My parents! Anselm!
SRILANKA: Go to my cabin in Vermont. Take your
parents. I'll tell you where to go.
SEAMAN: And their partner—their fellow subversive—
is the tailor who made this suit, whose name is
Anselm Kassar, and he has been making suits for
presidents and leaders from his atelier, Anselm de
Paris, on Sixty-Seventh Street between Fifth and
Madison, for years. And probably spying, probably
spying on everyone.
(*His pants suddenly fall to his ankles*)
But the *real* enemy is actually here tonight. The
representative of your worst fears, folks, the one
who will confirm everything you ever thought
about how profoundly the game is rigged against
you.
(*beat*)
Right now on my website—in one minute—you can
hear the audiotape of the chairwoman of my party

offering me five billion dollars to walk away from you, to betray you! The elites! The elites! That's your enemy! I stand before you virtually naked to tell you—the Second Civil War begins tonight. From coast to coast I have heard your . . . *despair* at the lies you were fed. And when *she* offered me five billion dollars to betray you, I finally knew that you, my friends, my dear, dear friends—you don't have any chance in America as it currently stands.

(*beat*)

So, we're going to have to start over, but first, as a wonderful lady named Maggie Dodelson said to me, "We're gonna have to burn the motherfucker down!" Let's begin the revolution tonight. Let's dispatch the enemies of America with God's own fury, let's salt the land with the bonfires of our wrath and brighten the skies with the embers of all the self-interested elites who have brought America to her knees—from within!

(*beat*)

Go to my website, Seaman dot com, and listen to the audio and buy a hat, Seaman Rising—become one of us, the Real Americans. You are a force against the forces that conspire against you! I am Kurt Seaman, and I am never, ever going away! Thank you! God bless you all and God bless America.

(AMIR, SRILANKA, *and* ANSELM *are stunned. Silent.*)

SRILANKA (*urgent*): Get out of here as soon as you can. Please!

(*A GIANT CRASH of broken glass from offstage.*)

ANSELM: Too late. They're here. It's too late.

(*We hear a loud and deafening roar and then SILENCE and then the PING of the elevator as the lights go to black.*)

END OF PLAY

ACKNOWLEDGMENTS

The playwright would like to acknowledge the Ojai Playwrights Conference for giving him a home to workshop this play and so many others before it.

Printed in the USA
CPSIA information can be obtained
at www.ICGtesting.com
LVHW091147150724
785511LV00005B/588

9 780374 283599